LOVE ALONE
Will Never Be Enough

Raising Drug-Affected Children

S. WAHRHEIT

authorHOUSE®

AuthorHouse™
1663 Liberty Drive
Bloomington, IN 47403
www.authorhouse.com
Phone: 1 (800) 839-8640

Published by AuthorHouse   07/11/2018

ISBN: 978-1-5462-4208-6 (sc)
ISBN: 978-1-5462-4207-9 (e)

Library of Congress Control Number: 2018905795

Print information available on the last page.

This book is printed on acid-free paper.

DEDICATION

This book is dedicated to Miriam Thompson,
long time Medical Foster Parent,
dearest Friend and Mentor, and Foster Grandmother
to the children in this book.

CONTENTS

PREFACE

Why do we have to build so many more prisons? Why do we have more murders, rapes, grand larcenies? Why do we have a large number of people in prison for these crimes for which in reality they are not responsible? What is the underlying cause, not in all cases but in a huge number? It is the parents who pass on drugs to the child through their genetic material.

This book will show how children of polydrug parents cannot function rationally. Their ability to think rationally and make moral decisions is severely damaged and can't be rejuvenated. All the professionals in the world cannot fix them.

It is a sad state of affairs.

The gap for "normal" behavior widens as the polydrugaffected child grows into adulthood. He or she cannot function socially, economically or morally in an acceptable manner and often ends up in prison. The justice system has no choice.

What is the best solution? Get rid of the drugs? How? God only knows. Easier said than done.

INTRODUCTION
My History

I am the second oldest of seven children growing up in a large Roman Catholic family. Working parents necessitated older children helping with the three youngest members. Diapering, feeding, cleaning, entertaining, teaching, supervising, sometimes hearing first words and seeing first steps were all part of being a member of a large family. I witnessed the home birth of one of my brothers and to this day have not forgotten any of the details involved in this wondrous event.

My family experiences have helped me greatly in raising my three adopted children. I don't know firsthand the labor pains a biological mother experiences, but I will tell you, adopting has its own set of pains. In addition to my upbringing, my career as a teacher and counselor has guided me and educated me in the ways of children. Classes in early childhood development, play, art and music therapy, and adolescent theories have all given me a deeper understanding of children and adolescents. Parents and teachers do not know everything about children, but if they keep an open mind and loving heart they can learn volumes from children.

A key element in working with children is to keep them involved in planning and developing ways to improve behaviors, attitudes, skills, and work ethic.

Some helpful hints: "This is my first time around as a parent and your first time as a child, so let's work together. We can learn together."

I used to hang a paper inside my kitchen cupboard to help me work on areas I needed to improve or change. As I was reading the sheet one day while drinking a glass of water, my six-year-old said, "Is that one of those new things you are learning?"

"Yes," I said, "we all need to learn. I can learn from you, and you can learn from me." Be a model for your children. They do what they see you do, not what you say.

CHAPTER 1
Wanting a Family

In 1968 I stood in my classroom on the third floor of our high school. I had just finished teaching a home economics class in sewing. I remember Melinda, a beautiful slim girl with large blue eyes and long silky light brown hair. She had eagerly finished a turquoise blouse. It looked gorgeous and would accentuate her kind blue eyes. The bell rang and the students drifted out. It was break time.

I collected my notes and gazed out the window to the campus below where students were milling about. I saw tinfoil flashing as they passed drugs. It hit me: These were the parents of tomorrow's children. I looked again; there was Melinda. "Oh no," I thought, "such a beautiful junior and getting into that." It was a Catholic high school, and the authorities worked hard to keep drugs out, but they got in. Standing there as a nun in a long black habit I had no inkling at that time that I would leave this order, marry a fine man and adopt three children whose parents had been heavy on drugs, children whose brains were permanently damaged, children who would face many obstacles ahead. I had no idea that my first little boy would have Melinda's beautiful blue eyes, fair complexion and light brown hair.

The wind rustled the maple trees lining the street. A warm sun beat down. I glanced again at the campus. Foil was still flashing. Sad!

Drugs reigned. I ached for the students who were bringing such doom on themselves and for the administration, who worked so hard not to have drugs on the campus. It was an impossible task. The culture made drugs the in-thing. No lecture, no program, no gifted speaker could stop them. Free will reigned. "Try it: you'll feel good." And they tried it.

Standing there that day I didn't realize what far reaching devastating effects drugs can have. Later when I was teaching in a high school, a young boy, Aaron, seventeen, tall, 6' 4," an excellent football player with muscles to spare, decided a few drugs would make his game even better. God only knows what combination he took. At seventeen he ended up in a care home, mute. Aaron had everything but wanted more, and now the medical team that works with him cannot reverse his situation. He cannot tie his own shoes or feed himself. I want to cry when I think about him, so young, so talented, with all those muscles going to waste and a good brain wrecked for life.

Later after we were happily married we wanted children, and since we couldn't have our own we looked at adoption. My wonderful husband, Marcos, was Peruvian. We visited his family in Peru. Walking in the streets we saw many beautiful children who were homeless, scrounging for food, dirty, half-clad and begging. My heart went out to them, as did my husband's, but we discovered that adopting from a foreign country involved many problems and red tape. So we looked to the United States. A friend who was a medical foster care person helped us.

At that time in the '70s it was not the policy to give out any information about the child's past, much of which was unknown. We soon found out that children come with mountains of unknowns. My friend helped us get a beautiful chubby cheeked, blue-eyed boy with sandy hair, Tony.

The first day at our house he sat on the basement stairs and wailed, "Mommy! Mommy!' There were no tears, just a steady plaintive cry.

I sat down beside him. I wanted to cry. My heart was breaking. *What sort of hell have these children been through?* I wondered. I put my arm around his shoulders. He didn't stop. He kept it up for a good five minutes. I said, "You want your mommy, and I'm not your mommy, but you are going to be our forever child!" Then I took him to the kitchen and gave him a snack and put my arm around him. He was quiet. I assured him again, "You are our forever little boy."

Later we took him to the basement play area; he was by the fireplace playing with a truck. Marcos and I were watching. Suddenly he picked up the truck and threw it at me. I dodged, and it missed.

Marcos got up, strode over to the fireplace, picked up Tony by his shoulders so they were face to face, looked him square in the eye, and said, "Don't you ever throw anything at your mom again!" He said it with such firmness and love that it never happened again, although Tony had a temper and did throw things.

Before we got Tony, we had scheduled a trip to Los Angeles, which included visits to Disneyland, Sea World, the zoo, etc. My husband's parents were coming from Peru to visit us for the first time. Tony arrived four days before this scheduled trip, so we took him with us. He was two and half years old, in the middle of potty training. I knew that change can be upsetting, so I took diapers with us.

Tony screamed non stop when I put him on the changing table. And he kept it up. In fact, he got worse. I kept telling him it was all right, but he couldn't for some reason feel safe. He did the screaming thing on escalators. In fact, he did a number of things that were not normal for his age. When we fed him he just kept stuffing food in, like a starved animal. He behaved very differently from children I had cared for, including my nieces and nephews. I had to give him little bits of food or drink or he would upchuck everything.

We visited Sea World in California. Tony couldn't handle any rides that went up and down. Heights bothered him. But he loved the fish. One time he got away from me, and I was sure he was going to jump in with the whales! We got splashed a lot, and Tony giggled and laughed.

We stayed in a nice hotel and went swimming in the pool. The first time, Tony started to pull off his swimsuit. "No, no, this is not a bath; leave it. And don't pee in the water." He loved the water. And it was fun.

I couldn't help but wonder what had happened to him, because he had so much terror doing simple things. He had a lot of trouble sleeping. When we got back home he kept up these behaviors. He would wake up screaming. I tried to soothe him. Sometimes when I wrapped him in a blanket it helped; he wouldn't let me cuddle him or do any of the things that usually quiet a child.

I thought back to the first day we brought him home. Imagine bringing home your darling little two-and-a-half year- old boy and he immediately goes to his carpeted room and stakes out his territory by peeing in every corner. I couldn't believe my eyes. "What do I have, a cat or child? Dear Lord, this really scares me. What next?"

I called the adoption worker and asked her about these behaviors. She said, "Give it time, and hopefully things will get better." I called my medical foster parent friend and asked her if she knew anything about Tony's history. She said both parents were drug users. After visiting with her I began to put pieces together, realizing I was not just dealing with adoption loss issues. I was dealing with a drug-affected child.

Research helped me know that you can't handle this kind of child like an ordinary child. It is necessary to go through all the stages of child development, such as crawling and rolling over. This helps with bonding, but it will never be like the real thing between a biological mother and child.

I remember Tony riding his tricycle in our driveway one day, hitting against the brick wall between the garage doors as hard as he could. I went out and asked, "Tony, what are you doing?"

"It's fun hitting the wall!"

"Let's find a place where you can ride without hitting."

I took him to the sidewalk and watched him to be sure he was safe.

Research had showed me that crack-affected children have smaller heads and have trouble bonding. They cannot handle being touched or looked at. Because bonding is so crucial to child development, a foster parent must supply it.

I went through all the stages of child development, crawling, rolling over, etc. This helped with bonding. It will never be perfect, but it is possible to make it much better. It was encouraging to know Tony did better after those play sessions.

In one family I know, not drug-affected, the big sister, about fifteen, was babysitting her little brother, David, about three. He was acting up, so she threatened him, "If you do that once more I will flush you down the toilet." He believe her and refused to go to the bathroom.

When their mom got home and found out the problem, she told her daughter, "Never, never, threaten anything you can't or won't do." This is key to raising any child.

CHAPTER 2
Rough Beginnings

All three of our adopted children had very rough beginnings in life. In this chapter we will try to point out some of these difficulties they had in coping.

Tony was born in February 1976 to drug-taking parents. He was often left to fend for himself. The police who took him from his abusive parents found a screaming undernourished baby, in a dirty diaper at least three days old, with a nasty rash on his little behind and down his legs. As an infant he was placed in foster care. His foster mother loved him, and he began to live again. He was held and nurtured and let know that he didn't have to scream for hours to get a little food or a clean diaper. His foster parents were expecting a child of their own, so he was returned to foster care.

This is where we came in and adopted Tony at two and a half years old. He was a beautiful child with big blue eyes, blond curly hair, and a smile we couldn't resist. Tony didn't want to leave his foster home. It was a sad parting. He felt ousted by the new baby coming, so apparently in his mind babies were bad. Whenever we visited a family with a baby in a crib I had to watch Tony carefully or he would dump the baby out of the crib or pour milk from the baby's bottle all over it. He was very sneaky and did it when no one was watching. These babies were his enemies so he wanted to get rid of them.

Tony had a real fear of heights. He would scream at the top of an escalator and have a panic attack if placed on a diaper-changing station. This could have come from being placed in a high place at night and left alone to fall to the floor. When the police took him he had terrible bruises.

He screamed anytime we got near something high. Just to stand on a porch and look out would give him the shudders. We had to hold him and keep assuring him that he was going to be all right. Babies affected by drugs have different needs. It has to do with brain damage.

As adoptive parents it was difficult to find Tony's early history because his files were spotty. We did see a police report and discovered he suffered from malnutrition, lactose intolerance, allergies and ear infections. We were glad to know about these so we could deal with them.

Tony was partly potty trained, but I knew he could regress, so in any strange situation I came supplied with diapers. This paid off when traveling. There were many fears and incidents in his early life that were hard to explain. Drugs leave a very bad trail of problems. Even after years of carefully monitored guidance problems arose, such as the following.

At five and six Tony was telling people who were smoking that they were going to die from cancer. At nine, Tony was finding and picking up used cigarettes off the street and smoking behind the bushes.

When Tony was ten he was home and I was at a meeting. He went to get a drink and hit the water faucet wrong. It went over the counter and out of the sink with water spilling out. He was terrified and couldn't turn it off. He panicked and called me. His IQ was 147 but he could not get calmed down enough to push it over the sink and turn it off. It took ten minutes to calm him. Why? Because that part of his brain did not function, a sad result of drugs.

As the child gets older problems are manifested in different ways. When Tony was fourteen he dropped a heavy Skate board ramp down the side of his leg and tore the flesh off so the bone was showing. He came into the house and said, "Mom, I need a Band-Aid." I took one look, told him to lie down, wrapped a clean wet towel around the leg, packed it with ice, and took him to the hospital.

These children can look normal, but they cannot act normal. The damage does not go away. It just comes out in different ways. Even as adults they cannot function socially or economically in an acceptable manner.

When Tony was fifteen he had gotten in trouble, and the judge put him in a treatment center for adolescents. After he came home he was lying on his bed crying, and he said to me, "I wish I could go away again and come back out of your tummy so I wouldn't have all these problems with drugs!"

I looked at Tony, and two tears slipped down my cheeks. My heart said, "Dear God, what has our society done to innocent children? What a sad heritage we give them by using drugs. How unfair!" I gave Tony a hug and said, "I wish you could have been my real child too." He tried to smile, but it was a very sad smile.

When we adopted Tony we had a six-month foster adopt, which meant his biological parents had six months to get their act together, to get drug and alcohol treatment, get a stable home, get a real job and be able to support a child, and get some counseling at a mental health clinic. They failed to meet any of the requirements, so our adoption of Tony was finalized.

At the end of those six months, when Tony was three, we got a call from the agency asking if we wanted a three year-old girl whose mother was giving her up, asking that she be put in a Christian home. We had one week to decide after our initial visit at the agency. We asked to meet this girl. We prepared Tony, explaining that he might have a little sister. Terri was a tiny three-year-old, very small for her age, weighing about twenty-nine pounds. Her fuzzy Afro hair was bigger than she was.

When we met her at the adoption agency, Tony walked up to her and said, "I don't like you. Go back home."

Her lips quivered, but she didn't cry, just stood there trembling. I picked her up and gave her a hug and said, "This is my Husband, Marcos. I'm Mariah, and this is Tony." She relaxed a little. The agency asked if we wanted to take her out for a day. We agreed.

She seemed comfortable with us, but I could see she was keeping everything inside. Her mother had given her up so many times before that there was hardly any trust left.

We did fun things. We asked her what she wanted to eat. "A hotdog on a stick and ice cream." We ate and went to a park. She had fun on the swings and merry-go-round while Tony watched. We fed the ducks and walked around the river.

After this first visit, which went very well, we got a call to see if we wanted her for an overnight visit. After that visit we sat down together and prayed and discussed. There were many tears; it was a tough decision. We decided yes. We went back to the agency to finish the paper work and finalize the adoption.

We told Tony, "Terri is going to be your sister."

The two played nicely together while we did the paperwork. That was a relief. But before they started playing with the toys in the corner, I could see the wistful look on her face. "Are you going to leave me too?" Her trust level was zero. We got in the car with two car seats and put them in. Big tears rolled quietly down her cheeks. I undid the car seat straps and put her on my lap.

We assured Tony from the day we brought him home that we were his forever parents. We assured Terri also. But she was hyper vigilant. She couldn't sleep. Our bedroom door was open, and so was her bedroom door. She seemed to question, "Am I safe?" It took a long time for Terri to have that fear leave her eyes.

When a child is hyper vigilant she has not had a safe predictable pattern in her early life. A child moved repeatedly to different homes or schools lacks a sense of security or accountability. Her well-being is shattered. Security is gone. Limits help her to feel loved and safe. It took Terri two years to feel safe. After two years she really believed she wouldn't be sent away.

She liked fluffy pink dresses and pretty things. She wanted to be our little princess, and we tried to help her feel at home. We told her we had some names picked out for her if she wanted a new name. She chose Theresa, and so she became Terri.

What we didn't know was that she had been sexually abused by her mother's boyfriend, who was dark skinned like my husband, so Terri cried whenever Marcos picked her up. She couldn't relate to him. She wanted to. I could see it in her eyes as she watched Marcos and Tony playing and roughhousing together.

Terri wanted to do everything right so she wouldn't be sent away. One day the furnace man came, and when I opened the door, she panicked and grabbed me around the leg. "You are not going to let him take me away!"

"No, no," I replied. "I'm your forever mommy, remember? This is the furnace man; he will not come in the house. He has to fix the furnace in the basement." Relief flooded her fearful eyes, and she gave me a quick hug.

Every time we went to visit at a friend's house, I had to carefully assure her that she was not going to be left behind. Sometimes she would say, "You're not going to leave me, Mommy, are you?"

"No, you're my forever girl." She loved the movie *Annie* and would ask me to play it again. She related to that. She liked orphan and animal stories and fairytales.

We had a sand tray that the children played in with a screen to cover it to keep cats out. I looked out one day to see Terri gagging because Tony was feeding her sand. They were doing make-believe eating, but he was getting too real. I rushed down there and cleaned the sand out of her mouth. Never a dull moment.

They loved the water, and we had a little pool in the backyard. Perhaps the lack of structure was what appealed, so fluid, so free. They were happiest outdoors, whether in the pool or in the woods.

Terri kept her room very tidy and nice. Tony didn't. He would go in and mess up her room and take the heads off her dolls. I explained, "We don't break other people's toys."

When she was getting new ones, Tony got none. He often had to learn things the hard way.

When Terri was five she asked, "Mommy, can I do dance?" so I took her to see ballet and tap and jazz. Ballet was too slow, so she settled for tap and was very good at it. She did tap dancing from five years of age until she was seventeen. She tried out for the Blazer dance troupe, but she wasn't tall enough. Dance and earning trophies became her life goal.

Tony liked gymnastics, so we enrolled him in that. It was a great outlet for his unbounded energy. We felt as parents a great responsibility to help each child find his or her giftedness and develop that, since we became acutely aware that with the drawbacks their biological parents had given them by using drugs they would need all the help they could get. It did pay off.

Terri came home from school one day and asked me, "Mommy, what is black? One girl in my class said, 'You're black, and I don't like you.'"

I said, "Let's look in the mirror." We did. "What color are you?"

"I'm not black; I'm brown."

"What color am I?"

"You're peachy."

"What color is Daddy?"

"He's chocolate."

"OK, honey, you're my little chocolate drop." And I gave her a kiss.

"Thank you, Mommy."

The third child we adopted was Eddie, Tony's biological brother. He was a year younger than Tony. Eddie was a failure-to-thrive baby, which means as a tiny infant he had given up on living and wanted to die, having been neglected and left hungry and cold. Failure-to-thrive babies will not look at you or eat or babble. They have totally given up because no one held them, talked to them, cuddled them, or took care of their basic needs. All they want is out, and they will die if not given a lot of extra love and care. This is what the medical foster parent, Miriam, did for Eddie. She kissed him. She talked to him. She cuddled him. She put the heart to live back in him.

Before we got Eddie he was in another home where they had two children who were mean to him. They were older and teased him and gave him a bad time. They plain didn't want him. It was a hard existence. They sent him back to Miriam, the one who had loved life back into him. This was after six months with this other family.

Tony met Eddie at a Christmas party at Miriam's house. I explained to Tony, "He's your for-real brother." After a couple of home visits we completed Eddie's move to our home. He loved Miriam, so we arranged for her to be Grandma Miriam. This worked well. It helped give him some roots.

Tony and Eddie shared the same room. They had bunk beds but not on top of each other. Tony didn't accept Eddie's place in our home and told him, "You need to go back to Grandma Miriam's house. I don't want you in my room!"

Eddie's eyes got big, and he stepped back and stood there looking quite bewildered. He didn't cry, but he looked ready to.

I stepped in. "Eddie, this is your brother, Tony. You are not going back to Grandma Miriam. This is your room and your home. You are our forever child." I gave a him a big hug and took him into the kitchen for a popsicle. I didn't look at Tony.

Later I spent some time with Tony and explained, "Eddie is your brother, and he is going to live here." Tony caught on gradually that he needed to share. They had many differences but learned to get along and to this day are very close.

Two weeks later I had Eddie alone in the car to get some shoes and clothes. Marcos had the other two. Eddie was in the back seat, two years old, scolding, "No! No! No! Nathan, don't do that!" He kept this up for a long time.

When we got to the store I sat down beside him and asked, "Eddie, who is Nathan?"

"Nathan bad, really bad!" I found out later that Nathan was Eddie's name in the other adoptive home. He was remembering the negative put-downs of his other home.

When we got home, I asked Eddie, "Do you want to play in the dollhouse with me?" I let him play and act out Nathan. He acted out the two older children who had given him a bad time at the last home. He was a very troubled, angry boy who broke things and threw stuff for apparently no reason except that there was too much hurt stored up inside him and it had to come out.

When Eddie was three we went to a program in Miriam's church with all three children. Partway through the service, Eddie pulled on my arm. "What's the matter?" I asked.

"Bad people behind us!"

"Bad people?"

"Very bad!" I found out the family who had him for six months and didn't like him was sitting behind us.

Later when we went out to eat after the program I told Eddie, "You never have to see those people again." He gave me a little hug and seemed satisfied. Eddie was language delayed. He could talk, but it took him longer and he was not as fast and skilled as his big brother.

Eddie was my climber. He figured out ways to get up on things he wanted to investigate. One day at four years old he was covered in peanut butter and jelly sitting atop the kitchen counter. I asked him, "What are you doing?"

He replied, "Making a mess."

If there was a spot of water anywhere Eddie was on it. If he could turn on the water, he was up to his ears in it. We put a pool in our backyard, hoping to give all our children a safe place for water play, but it didn't last more than one day. He and his brother, Tony, decided to throw screwdrivers at the sides of it until all the air was let out and the ground was saturated with water. Each day was a new discovery and adventure somewhere in our yard or house.

One day when I checked on my children on the backyard play set, five-year-old Eddie was crawling across the top of the jungle gym bar, pushing the limits of how high he could go, with no fear. He would climb the highest trees in the yard and hide things like food or toys and other items he should not be playing with in the branches so he could retrieve them later.

At six Eddie also liked to disappear and be gone for several hours. There were only so many places in the neighborhood he could go, so we would soon find him. Sometimes he could not be found, but eventually he found his own way back home.

After spending an entire morning wallpapering his room with cartoon characters, I found cuts in the characters. Puzzled, I said, "Eddie, how did these marks get on the paper?"

"Easy," he said. "I was throwing this Chinese star to see if it would stick to the wall."

"And what did you find?" I asked.

"Easy, Mom. See the marks? It stuck really good."

Seven was a more adventurous year. Eddie was very good at finding lots of things that were not his. When we visited our relatives or friends or a store, I always had to do a bathroom frisk before we left. I was amazed at what and where both Eddie and Tony could hide things on their bodies. Ever-watchful eyes and ears were needed with this crew. This behavior lasted well into their teen years.

After putting my husband's good polyester pants and shirts in the dryer, I went to prepare dinner. One hour later when I went to check on the clothes in the dryer, I found that one of my little angels had put a handful of crayons in the dryer while it was going. As I removed the clothes and proceeded to hang them up, I found a rainbow of colors on everything. Thank goodness I was able to get all the melted crayon off all the clothing. So many creative surprises!

All three had very rough beginnings, but we hoped with consistent love and careful daily help to get these three into some form of more normal behavior. It was not going to be easy, and many challenges faced us, but armed with prayer and ordinary common sense we went ahead. We rejoiced over even small successes. We remained positive in many frustrating situations. I personally felt God was with us because we never, ever, tried to do it on our own. I believe I prayed more as a mother than I ever did as a nun. And I know God heard me.

CHAPTER 3
Uncooking a Hard-Boiled Egg

A key factor in a child's development is bonding with the parents, especially the mom, in early years. This occurs naturally in a healthy mother-child relationship, but in drug-affected children it often doesn't happen. It is blocked. And it gets more blocked because often the mother is too busy with drug paraphernalia to hold or cuddle or feed her child. Often the child is left in a soiled diaper screaming for food. Neglect plays a terrible role in drug-affected children, whether it be street drugs or alcohol or any combination.

This child ends up without an interior locus of control. He finds it difficult to make choices appropriate to his age level. His emotional needs for affection, comfort, and stimulation have not been met. The area of the brain for conscious decision-making has not been developed. So the child has to learn from the outside in.

Adoptive parents or foster parents have to put on all the controls. To heal the child's central nervous system is like trying to uncook a hard-boiled egg. It just won't work. So the adults in the picture have to work around this. It takes undying patience and lots of skill.

I learned early in the lives of our three that we had to provide all the guidelines and control. No easy task. And it was impossible for them to make transitions smoothly, so we had to practice for any kind of change.

For example, if we were going to church we sat down and went through what we did in church. "We sit quietly. We color our Bible storybooks or look at them. We talk quietly to Jesus or watch the priest."

One Sunday Tony kept thumping the kneeler. I picked him up and carried him out. He kept yelling, "No, Mama, no, Mama. I wanna go to church!" The people heard him and tried not to laugh out loud. I smiled and walked to the back of the church.

I sat for five minutes in the car and then asked him, "Now do you think you can do what we do in church?"

"Yes, Mama."

I had to be extremely consistent. My husband and I always had to do what we said we would, and of course it had to be something we *could* do. This was a great help.

Car protocol called for leaving the seat belt on. If one of them couldn't manage this we turned around and went back home and called the sitter and took the other two wherever we were headed. I don't believe in physical force; I think it only teaches children to be violent. Nor did I yell at them. Two people out of control doesn't work. Timeouts worked well. When they were small it was two or three minutes, and it didn't start until they were sitting quietly. Sometimes it took twenty minutes until they were able to stop hollering, but in the end we got results. I had timers all over the house.

We took time to go through what was appropriate in each part of the house. Only one person in the bathroom at a time. This eliminated throwing water at each other and horseplay.

As I mentioned earlier, correct behavior in stores was very carefully observed. One time I had my grocery cart full when Eddie couldn't manage to keep his hands off the cookies. I found the manager and asked him to keep my cart of groceries, took the kids home, got the sitter for Eddie, and went back with the two who could manage and finished. The manager said he wished more moms would be like me. He said it would make his job a lot easier.

All three learned what was appropriate. One time before Eddie could speak clearly he said, "Mama, Tony's not being 'propriate." He was jumping on the bed. But a time-out in the hallway took care of it.

Whenever we planned to go to a movie I had two or three plans in case one didn't work because of the difficulty these children had with transitions. So if the theatre showing Walt Disney's *Cinderella* was full we knew ahead of time we would go eat pizza and shop a bit or have some other type of outing. This saved a lot of screaming and lack of smooth transitions. It also saved on babysitter bills.

We practiced for company ahead of time. No horseplay. No throwing things. I took a good twenty minutes before company came to sit down and practice appropriate behavior. It paid off. They could not function as normal children due to brain damage. We had to put all the brakes on in a gentle, firm, loving way. It worked but was exhausting. There were so many holes in the walls. I used to buy plaster in a five-pound bag and became a pro at patching.

My husband bought a lovely play set with a swing, slide, and jungle gym. They loved to play on it but would fight over who got to be first, so we rotated it and then did it by drawing numbers. Drawing numbers worked for car seat places too, which could be a very hot issue. I made them each a denim bag with their name on it for car trips. They could take whatever fit in the bag, but they couldn't ever throw stuff in the car. I also used tickets for right behavior. I used different colors for each child so no one could swipe someone else's ticket. If you could stack up five you got a penny for your piggybank. This worked well when they were five, six, and seven years old.

Many adopted children suffering from in-utero drug and alcohol abuse end up with reactive detachment disorder. This clinical term means they never bonded with their mother and have trouble developing social awareness because their early needs for comfort, affection, and stimulation were not met. A child born of drug-using parents who is neglected will scream and cry for food or a diaper change. When no one comes he will give up and turn off all adults. He will begin to self-parent.

Studies have shown this situation cannot be totally reversed. It can be helped. This child will have a "rubber conscience" and will do what fits, creating his own truths. (We call it lying.) He will lie, cheat, steal, and look out for himself and no one else. He cannot form good bonds with adults. Being totally irresponsible he will break the law and often land in jail. It becomes a terrible cycle.

A grown adult with reactive detachment disorder will have a melt down/tantrum in a situation like a messy house or a meal not ready on time or clean clothes not available. He will act irrational and start screaming and throwing things in a very immature way instead of pitching in and remedying the situation. He lacks the ability to be an adult. That part of his brain has been permanently affected.

This business of creating one's own truths does not fit in our "normal" society and naturally causes grave problems, which our society fixes by locking them up, running out of jail space.

In my family situation I found that my three children could learn some adaptive behaviors. It will not always carry over into adulthood, but it does have some good effects.

The nice part was that the consistency paid off. All three began to see the rewards of doing what was appropriate. For example, when we went to *Costco*, which they loved to do, all three managed to follow the rules so they could partake of the many food edibles being offered. We would buy them something they liked, such as animal crackers. They enjoyed eating them on the way home.

Even though consistency most times paid off, we did not have the luxury of appropriate behavior 100 percent of the time. Learning from their mistakes is most difficult for drug-affected children because without a conscience they cannot internalize values or rules.

CHAPTER 4
Choices

Consistency is the key factor in raising any child and even more so in drug-affected children. When my son Tony was nineteen he said to me, "Mom, you always did what you said." And that is not easy to do. Sometimes it was downright inconvenient.

One example happened when they were about five to seven years old. We were going to go have ice cream after they got their rooms picked up. Charts on the wall showed what needed to be done:

toys in toy chest

soiled clothes in laundry hamper

books on shelf

They needed to have the room ready for me to vacuum. There was a timer set in each room to help the process.

Tony refused to pick up his room. We went to Baskin Robbins, got our ice cream and sat down and ate it while Tony sat and watched us with no ice cream. I imagine that most parents would consider this a cruel and unusual consequence, but with children as drug damaged as ours, tough love was the only way they learned. It only happened once.

As I mentioned earlier, these children lost out on going through the early childhood developmental stages, so I made a game of it. We rolled on the floor. We sat up. We crawled. This was at three years old. These steps are vital to physical and mental growth. Correct development would help them later make age-appropriate choices and learn to respect each other's space.

Boundary skills needed constant reinforcement and teaching. To help them understand each other's space I used hula-hoops and large appliance boxes. The area inside the hoop was their private space. I explained how each person needs private space. God made us social yet individual. They like the idea of their own private space. I cut doors in the boxes and printed their names on each one's house. Permission was needed to enter another's house.

I began early on helping them make choices. Tony was sitting in his high chair with an empty cereal bowl in front of him. I held a box of Cheerios in one hand and a box of Kix in the other. "Which do you want?"

"I want both of each."

I put the Kix in the cupboard and asked, "Which do you want, the empty bowl or the bowl with Cheerios in it?" He got wise and chose the Cheerios. Not choosing was not an option.

It is most important to work with your spouse as a team and never let the child play one against the other, as Tony was so skillful in doing. Set the limit and never back down.

Tony spilled some cornflakes on the kitchen floor. I asked him to sweep them up. "I don't want to."

My husband was taking a nap. Tony walked into the other room and started screaming and making a big tantrum. Marcos woke up. "What are you doing to him?"

"Just asking him to clean up his mess."

He turned to Tony. "Clean it up." When Tony realized his daddy wasn't going to rescue him he swept up the cornflakes.

Marcos and I had many conferences behind closed doors on how to handle situations. We agreed never to talk about the kids in front of them and to present a united front. If we didn't agree on how to handle some situation we would say to the child, "I will get back to you." We also had some buzz words for each other, like an SOS. If either one of us came upon a situation and saw we were in over our heads, we would say to our spouse, "Please, I need some help here."

Children with very limited understanding of boundaries and a poorly formed conscience have a great deal of trouble respecting others' property and possessions. If they see something they want, they take it, even if it is something they can't use or don't need. In order to prevent our children from acquiring other people's things we had to lock doors and cupboards in our own home.

Marcos hated all the locked doors. Purses, wallets, and freezers had to be locked. Our bedroom door had to be locked. I felt like a jailer with a bundle of keys hanging at my waist. We realized early that these children could not function as normal children, so we had to set all the limits. We resolved with a commitment as strong as our marriage bonds that we would work with what we had in these children, "for better or for worse, for richer or for poorer, in sickness and in health, until death do us part." Sometimes we wondered who would die first.

We looked at the children we had adopted and reset our expectations to match what they were. This was not an easy task, because parents always have high expectations for their children. Expecting them to grow and behave as normal was not a realistic expectation for us. We tried to put no expectations on them that they could not meet. This alone relieved a lot of tension and heartache.

When they were in grammar school I used a list system with three levels of jobs. We sat down together and figured out what should be on the lists. First level were easy jobs, second a little harder, and third, hardest. Cleaning the bathroom was a number three job. One had to scrub the floor, scrub the tub, clean the toilet, hang up fresh towels, and make sure to clean the mirror. If the children needed money for a small item, say a pad of paper or a pencil, they could earn it by doing a number one job. If they needed something bigger, like movie money, a number two might work, and if they needed something bigger, like a new radio, a down payment on a new bike, or a skateboard, a number three would do.

We used the same lists for managing inappropriate behavior. For example, if they didn't come home directly from school and went to a friend's house without checking, we sat down and asked, "OK, what list do we need?" They liked this system because they never got yelled at. For high school we added to and subtracted from the lists with their input.

For example, if they were fifteen minutes late they lost half an hour off the next outing. If they were more than an hour late they missed the next date.

This consistency paid off. We were able to take them on family outings and received many compliments from strangers on how well behaved they were. Disneyland was a fun trip. They were exuberant about the rides, the wilder the better. Tony hollered, hanging upside down on the Loop de Loop, "Look, Mom, I'm in outer space! Don't you want to try it?"

"Thanks, I'll watch from here."

Even Terri screamed in delight as the Octopus whirled her up and down in every direction. Eddie loved the Giant Spinner. It seemed like the higher, the faster, and the more daredevil it was, the better they liked it. Marcos and I held hands and watched, grateful that God was helping us raise these disadvantaged yet beautiful children.

These children had some normal times. Eddie was very creative and would make up little shows and plays and sing. Now as an adult he is still involved in drama. Terri and Tony also behaved as regular children some of the time. As I look back it makes me sad to think of the terrible damage parents can inflict on an unborn child by using drugs and alcohol.

Swimming and water sports were second nature to them. So Sea World was one of their favorite vacation spots. Watching the whales and porpoises and getting all wet delighted them. Eddie wanted to jump in and join the whales. "Daddy, I'm part whale!"

"No, you can't join them for a swim. Later at the motel you can swim!"

Often at night when we had all three tucked safely in we sat down together and prayed. We thanked God for Tony, with his sandy hair, gorgeous big blue eyes, and energetic self. We thanked God for Eddie, with his brown skin, deep blue eyes, and dark hair, and for Terri with her kinky black hair, brown eyes, and warm brown skin.

After they were grown up I explained to Tony how there were times when I longed for a spaceship. "Yes," I said, "there were times when I wanted to put you on the front porch and have a spaceship carry you away. I thought maybe if I just planted you there and asked God to send a spaceship all my troubles would be over."

"Oh Mom, I didn't know that!"

"Yes, there were other times when I thought about running away, but you see I didn't, because we had a loving commitment to God and to you to bring you up as best as we could. You didn't know that you weren't the only one who thought of running away."

"Gosh, Mom, I never ever thought of you doing that. So parents have tough times too."

"Some day if you are a parent, you will understand that there are some things you think about that you never do."

"Then Mom, how did you manage?"

"By a lot of prayer. Your father and I had to rely on God every inch of the way. The nice thing was, God got us through. We still thank God for helping us, and we pray for His angels around you every day."

CHAPTER 5
Creative Chaos

Children with in-utero drug damage to the brain do not have the ability to see the danger in a situation. Eddie liked fires and managed to get a stick of wood that he could poke into the furnace and make a torch so he could light up his world, much to the chagrin of his elders. He set so many fires at school I was surprised that he didn't get permanently expelled. It was a tough job keeping up with his fires.

Eddie and Tony stood at he window of the second floor and dropped toothpaste out of the tube onto the cement driveway below. Eddie made little globs and big globs. I said, "Tell me what you are doing."

"I just wanted to see how big a splash it would make."

"Well, now you have seen how it works, so you need to clean it up."

"I don't know how."

"In this family if you make a mess you have to clean it up. Come, I will show you how." He fussed. He squalled. But in the end he did clean it up.

One day Tony was rubbing something on the door between the house and garage. He was leaning out with his hand behind the door. I asked him what he was doing.

"I am tickling the door." I went out to look, and he had gouged big holes and scratches in the finish. He had a good imagination.

We sent Tony to special camp for attention-deficit children. He loved it and had a great time. Campfires especially intrigued him. Not long after that I arrived at our house one afternoon to find the place surround by firemen and fire trucks. Tony had built a large fire under a pine in the backyard. Never a dull moment.

At school both Tony and Eddie had to have their crayons, markers, pens, and scissors locked in the teacher's desk; otherwise the other children were in danger of being tattooed and decorated from top to bottom. Eddie loved to draw and knew no boundaries as far as where to draw. A little girl classmate came running to the teacher before the locking system was put into effect. "Mrs. Jensen, he drew a frog on my arm!"

In kindergarten Eddie gave the teacher a merry chase by crawling under the desks, pretending he was a dog, and nibbling on the children. There were giggles and pandemonium until the teacher discovered the source. Again, never a dull moment.

I was called to school very frequently to help with my three. At times I felt like a permanent fixture there. The good thing was that I also had a creative imagination most times and could stay one step ahead of them. But I have to admit, some of this crazy-making was wearing.

As they got older, Tony's bedroom and Eddie's were next to each other, and instead of going to the door to talk, they would poke a hole in the plaster and talk though the hole. As I mentioned earlier, I would buy plaster in large bags to keep the place looking livable.

Another bit of creative chaos was that these children would take food and leave the empty container on the shelf. It would look as if we had a box of Wheat Thins when the box was empty and carefully put back. It was a tricky business figuring out what was next. Locks became a necessity because their choice-making abilities were limited.

When they got bigger and couldn't pop the locks they would get a screwdriver and take the hinges off. Yes, it was a jolly game keeping one's sanity and staying ahead of all that was going on.

Many times Tony would say to me, "I'm going to kill myself."

I would say, "Oh, how are you going to do that?"

We were on the second floor, looking out over the garage. "I'm going to jump out this window and land on the cement."

"Then what are you going to do?"

"Lie there and see if anyone comes."

"And then?"

"If no one comes I will get up and dust myself off and come in the house." It seemed as if they often did things without thinking of the consequences.

Another time Tony was in the bathroom with the cord from the blind around his neck. He was trying to get it off and in the process kept making it tighter. When I found him he was standing on tiptoe, trying to breathe and having a miserable time. After I got him released I asked him what he was trying to do. "I wanted to see what it felt like."

"What did it feel like?"

"It didn't hurt at first, but when I tried to get out it got tighter and hurt my neck."

I asked, "Did you learn anything from this? Why did you do it?"

"I don't know; I just did it."

They cannot explain their impulsive, irrational behavior. They are brain damaged but not mentally challenged. And one sad part is that the gap between their chronological age and their mental age becomes wider as they grow up. The central nervous system is messed up; they simply do not connect.

When Eddie was about ten he tied a rope to his leg and climbed the tree in the backyard. I heard him yelling, "Help! Mom, help!"

I was in the house; I hunted in every room and finally located him outside, hanging from the tree by one leg with his head three inches from the ground.

I rescued him, and he couldn't tell me why he did it. It seems their brain pattern is so damaged they cannot see what is dangerous and will try anything.

Tony threatened to run away. "Go ahead," I told him. He got their little red wagon and loaded it with food, toys, and a few clothes. I said, "Hey, wait a minute. You can take only what is yours. The food and wagon belong here. The clothes are yours."

"OK." He left the wagon and went out and walked up and down the sidewalk. I watched him. Then he came back and said, "I'm hungry."

"Come on in; it's time for dinner."

When Tony was about eleven he started sniffing everything. We did a super job of locking paint cans and cleaning fluids in the basement, but he persisted in prying holes in the doors. One day after we had made model airplanes I collected the glue, but he managed to hide one bottle.

The next day the babysitter had them. Tony was acting strange; he couldn't breathe and he couldn't see. The sitter put him outside to get some air. My daughter called me. I said, "Call 911." They did.

I hurried home from work and arrived just as the ambulance did. They gave him oxygen and brought him back, just in time, or he would have additional brain damage.

One day I walked into the bathroom and thought, *What a strange musty smell is in here!* I investigated. I found two inches of water in each drawer. "Tony, what is going on in here?"

"Mama, I was floating my rubber ducks."

"See the bathtub?"

"Yes."

"That is where you float your rubber duckies. Now help me clean up this mess and put these out in the sun to dry."

Both boys were fascinated by sticky food, wet paper wads, anything that would stick to the ceiling. It was some sort of game that really held their interest. The aim of the game was to see who could make the most stick. My dear husband was most unfond of this game, and we ended up giving them number three on the list for this misdemeanor.

Scissors were a great invention for Eddie. His bedroom had some lovely sheer curtains. He cut long strips and various designs into them. "What are you doing?"

"Seeing if my scissors work."

"Oh. What did you find out?"

"They work."

"Those are your school scissors. What are they doing here?"

Silence. "Mom, I forgot to give them to the teacher."

"Eddie, I need the scissors." Then I called the school and told the teacher, "Eddie is returning the scissors."

I had a beautiful gold velvet chair. I walked in and discovered it covered with drawings done in black permanent marking pen. I sat them down and gathered some information on how the drawings got there.

Eddie admitted he had decorated the chair, and then he added, "But Mom, you have that good cleaning stuff. You can get it out!"

I took a look and said under my breath, "Please, God, send that spaceship." Yet most times I had to laugh under my breath at their creative ventures, because if I cried I might never have stopped.

CHAPTER 6
School Issues

Elementary school provides lots of information about the effects of polydrugs on children. It is also an eye-opener on how this interferes with normal relationships and learning.

Tony could not focus, sit still, keep his mouth quiet, or interact appropriately with teachers and peers. When a classmate did try to play or interact with Tony, he was unable to be a friend. He monopolized his peers and tried to own them and drove everyone away. After Tony was evaluated and put on medication he did better in the scholastic part of school, but connecting with friends was extremely difficult because he insisted on ownership and exclusive rights rather than sharing and being happy that his friend had other friends.

In first grade, Tony spent most of his time in the principal's office, talking, drawing, or basically climbing the walls. When I had him evaluated at six years of age, his IQ was 147, but he could not access his brain because of inutero drug damage. His learning style was hands on and very visual, not always the style of his teachers. He spent lots of time with learning specialists.

Eddie was not a noisy child at school; he would quietly crawl around a classroom and pretend he was a dog, gnawing at children's clothes, barking like a dog, and disrupting the class. In kindergarten he started doing his doggie behavior the first half-day of school, setting off the class and causing general havoc. His veteran kindergarten teacher of thirty years had to call me that day. Eddie was also evaluated and found to have an average IQ, but his language difficulties greatly interfered with understanding and processing information from teachers and peers. Eddie was also put on medication for his poor attention, which helped him to act more appropriately, but he needed lots of help from the speech and language therapist and the counselor. When he was sexually abused in the after-school daycare, his behavior and learning took a major nosedive.

Discrepancies between sound emotional and chronological growth widen in these children as they get older, so there is a much more noticeable difference in their ability to relate socially, emotionally, and mentally.

Eddie had difficulties understanding and translating language into his everyday world. He misread a lot of verbal and nonverbal communication. When overwhelmed by the schoolwork or verbal teaching style, he would just scoot his little body along the floor until he was near the door. Then he'd disappear down the hall and into the great outdoors. Sometimes he would entice a classmate to accompany him on his adventure. Eddie was great for doing the "disappearing act" at school and at home.

Terri's attention problems and language problems led her to being "Miss Social Butterfly." Anything was better than boring schoolwork. She was able to maintain friendships, but at great cost to her learning. She was constantly being embarrassed by her brothers' outlandish behavior at school and on the bus. She didn't want to relate to them. Terri was also in special classes for language and math and better focusing, since her attention span was limited.

Of my three children, Terri had more appropriate social skills and interactive behavior than her brothers. She had a number of friends, and her brother Tony took delight in trying to alienate them. He seemed to be perpetually jealous.

One time Terri brought Judy home, and they were playing with their dolls. Tony waited until Terri was out of the room getting a snack for them to tell Judy, "Terri said your hair looks awful. Why do you wear pigtails?" Judy looked crestfallen.

When Terri came back in Judy asked her, "Terri, did you tell Tony my hair looks awful?"

"No. I would never say a mean thing like that. Don't pay any attention to Tony. He has problems." And she gave her friend a hug.

Terri chose her battles and let the rest go. She managed not to get frustrated with her brother, but it did take some doing.

There were not any days without challenges. We learned as a family to be constantly aware and to meet each day and each new problem with more prayer and with confidence that comes only from relying on God.

CHAPTER 7

Teen Turmoil

Adolescent years for my children started at twelve as their bodies began to develop. Social and emotional behavior was off the wall. What was previously manageable magnified itself fifty times. "Crazy making" was the mode of the day.

It took longer to diffuse anger, emotional upsets, sibling squabbles, confrontations, school upsets, and friendship issues. We went back to the drawing board to update strategies for keeping behavior somewhat in balance.

Junior high was a nightmare in daytime for Tony. As teens and preteens were fighting for recognition, Tony was at the bottom of the pecking order due to his lack of awareness of social cues, facial expressions, innuendos, cliques, appropriate attire, or the latest attire.

The harder Tony tried to fit in, the worse it got. He ended up the butt of many dreadful pranks. Going to the bathroom was no longer simply routine. Two strong thugs grabbed him, forced his head in the toilet, and held him there while they flushed it. His clothing was ripped. And he was manhandled unmercifully. When issues were reported to authorities Tony was so angry and out of control he was unable to give an accurate report. He couldn't wait his turn to tell what happened, and this impulsive behavior got him deeper into trouble.

To diffuse a hot situation with teens it is important to stand between them, make them take fifteen deep breaths, and let them know you can't help them until they are calm. I witnessed a number of times when school counselors and authorities did not take into account the raging hormones of teens. Even normal teens, not messed up by drugs, need this sort of time-out before a situation can be resolved.

Tony was very verbal and very indiscreet. He said what came to his mind and by this behavior set himself up as a target for many cruel jokes. His lunchbox was taken and passed around, the goodies removed and replaced with garbage. Feces out of the toilet were placed in his locker. It was very rude, smelly behavior.

An example of Tony's lack of manners and appropriate speech happened on the street. "That lady should comb her hair!" He rarely considered his words before he spoke them. Or on another occasion, "What an ugly dress!" We tried hard to get him to remember not to say everything he was thinking.

Eddie did not have the same problems as his brother Tony because he did not shoot his mouth off. He was extremely good with his hands. He loved to take things apart and make them into something else. In one science lab he put a few things together and made a rocket that knocked out two fluorescent lights. Another time in shop he caught a girl's hair on fire with his project. Luckily she didn't suffer burns.

Neither Tony or Eddie could do team sports. They could not organize their thoughts enough to keep the rules straight and were not capable of team work. On a team Eddie would run to the opposite team's goal. So team sports were not an option. Gymnastics were great for Tony until he got kicked out for not following the safety rules. Swimming and water exercises worked best. Both enjoyed these, and all went well until Tony thought a girl in the pool looked at him in way he didn't like, so he slugged her. Her parents pressed charges. Tony felt he had to get even with the supervisor who reported him, so he put garbage in his car. We had to go to court.

The judge told him he had to obey the home rules, the neighborhood rules, and the school rules at all times. If not, I was to call the police.

One day at home while his dad was at work, he came walking down the hall. I could see he was very distraught and needed to calm down, so I said, "Tony, go to your room and calm down." He kept coming toward me. He looked stoned. I followed what the judge had said and called the police.

A tall policeman came immediately and asked, "Do you need help?"

"Yes, my son is not following the rules, and the judge said I should call you." He handcuffed him.

Tony was in Portland detention for one weekend. He cried all the time he was there. My husband asked him, "Why did you do that?" He could give no explanation. That is so true of drug-affected children. They just do things that are irrational and totally unexplainable.

A very difficult situation to handle was when Tony took revenge. When some of the boys in the neighborhood had done him in at school he gathered dog feces and put it on their back porch rails and on the porch and then lit a fire on the porch. Luckily he didn't manage to burn the house down.

Terri had better social skills than her brothers. She did a good job in middle school picking friends. Being attention deficit she was in special education. Language was a problem. She did her homework but didn't hand it in.

Terri could not talk about her problems. I would say, "Go draw me a picture." Then she would explain the picture, and we got to what was hurting. She was pretty and quite social; boys tried to get her into bed. This got worse as she got older. I have very good hearing, and one night I thought I heard the ringer on the back door go off in the middle of the night. I asked Marcos, who did not hear anything. The next morning as he was going to work at 6:30 a.m. he met Terri coming in.

"Where have you been?" he thundered. She had sneaked out and spent the night at a boy's house. She didn't tell him that but said, "We had a sleepover at school in the gym." She and Tony were very adept at making up a story to fit the occasion. She couldn't confront us, but we found notes saying she would like to kill both her parents.

Eddie had other problems as a teen. His body was very hairy, and he felt picked on in gym class when the boys all took showers together. He took to shaving it. He was small but good-looking. Later he wanted to be a model but wasn't tall enough. He was part Afro-American, and he didn't like the fact that as he became a teen his black wavy hair got kinky.

Eddie and Terri survived the teen years better than Tony. But actually it was a nightmare for all five of us, especially for my husband. We had to lean on God with all our might; there was no other way to go. And the biggest miracle of all is that there were multiple times when we could have been sued, but we never were.

CHAPTER 8
Parental Stress

Stress comes in a situation one cannot control. One can alleviate the circumstances but not the outcome. There was a huge amount of stress dealing with these drug-affected children.

How did I cope? I prayed first. I asked for one miracle after another.

I screamed, but never in front of the children. I cried. I beat the steering wheel sometimes when I drove and told God, "These are not children! They are not human beings! Do something about it."

I talked to my supportive husband, who had a hard time realizing they were truly not normal children. He didn't have my background in child therapy or counseling, so it was even more difficult for him. We prayed, struggled, and worked.

Perhaps what was most frustrating of all was that they rarely learned from mistakes. I would ask, "What did you learn from that?" Nothing. They came up blank.

After Eddie had helped Tony make a campfire in the backyard I came home to find our house surrounded by firemen. There was a huge fire under a dry pine tree. Nasty shock! When things were retuned to normal I asked, "What did you learn from that?"

Eddie looked at me, blank, and replied, "It sure made a lot of smoke." Eddie had to go to fire safety school, but that didn't stop his need to use fire. Eddie used fire to make something, for example, he saw wood burning done and was interested in that. He saw how wax was melted to make candles. He was not a pyromaniac. He wanted to use fire to make things. But his timing and choices were not the best.

"Do you realize you could have burned the house down?" Another blank stare.

All three were completely oblivious to danger. Because of brain damage they did not have any foresight. I realized I needed a more astute babysitter after the fire, and I also realized it was not possible to give them what they didn't have. So again, God help us.

When Tony was feeding Terri sand I could see there was no connection between reality and play. She was gagging, so I was glad I got her mouth cleaned out before she choked. "But Mom, we were just playing."

I could see even at this early age (three and four years old) it was going to be an uphill drive. My constant prayer was "God, I need Your help."

We looked for and tried various solutions. Some doctor prescribed medications seemed to help a little. One that Tony was on made him complain that he felt like there was something wrong with his head. He would hide medication in the heat register.

Another helpful factor was that we never, ever, put the children down. We worked on a positive approach and praised them for every slight improvement.

For a while I was physically run down from working so hard with these three; however, I was able to find a good chiropractor, who helped tremendously, and some vitamins and food that restored my physical, emotional, and mental equilibrium. I am very aware that to be physically fit is a great asset in any stress situation.

A sense of humor is always helpful. When I was at my wits' end and would step out on the front porch and beg God for a spaceship to whisk away the children, somehow I felt that God was listening hard and smiling down on me. My faith told me He had never abandoned me but together we would get through all this. Sometimes I would just hold my head and say, "Dear God, what have I gotten myself into?" Marcos and I prayed together every night often on our knees, sometimes together in bed. This was a vital part of raising these children. We were very aware that the problems were bigger than we could handle.

There is a true story of George Washington at Valley Forge when the war was going badly and the soldiers had no shoes. They were leaving bloody footprints in the snow, and they couldn't find Washington. Finally they found him in the woods, kneeling by a tree praying. He explained, "I have nowhere else to go but to God." I felt like that often.

When Tony was fourteen he was involved in many swimming activities. It was about the only sport he could handle. One time in the pool he didn't like the way a girl looked at him, so he hauled off and slugged her. We had to go to court over the ensuing mess. Talk about stress! This was enough to send one's blood pressure sky high. But God never let us down, and I know He never gives us more than we can handle—although there were many times when I would have preferred that spaceship handily parked on the front porch ready for liftoff.

There were smaller challenges, such as the time we went to a movie, and right about halfway through Tony said,

"Mom, can we have our popsicles now?"

"What popsicles?"

"The ones I put in your purse."

I looked. Horrors! My purse was floating. One factor that helped me tremendously in handling stress was that as a child I learned from my mother how to respond rather than react. Terri was a wonderful dancer, took lessons and did well, and thoroughly enjoyed it. As a six-year-old she was upstairs, and her dad was there too. She was dancing down the hall, got a bit rambunctious, and hit her elbow hard against the wall, breaking her arm so badly it hung down in the middle at a right angle. My husband started screaming, "Mariah, get up here! Something is wrong with Terri!"

Terri was in pain but was very quiet. Marcos reacted, and I responded. I went quickly upstairs, took in the situation, asked Tony to bring me two magazines and Marcos to bring me a towel. I reassured Terri, made a splint, and got her to the hospital. My early observance of how my mom handled emergencies helped me.

Another great stress reliever was our four-pound Yorkshire Terrier, Fifi. She was my best counselor. When I worked as a counselor at school I would bring Fifi, and she would go quietly around the group of children sitting on the floor listening to the story and sit by the most troubled one. She would sit quietly, and if the child looked at her she would put her paw gently on the child's leg. Then if the child smiled and patted her she would lay her head on the child's leg and then snuggle up in her arms and start giving loving licks. She seemed to understand where there was pain and hurt. Fifi helped lots of children, especially our three, for fifteen years. The unconditional love of an animal is a great cure for many ills.

When I was counseling other children I always asked God to take care of our own, who were at school. I had a tremendous principal who would allow me to go home in any emergency. He loved and understood children. He put families first.

When Eddie was fourteen he was banished from a store for stealing. First he would hide large candy bars on his person; then he would go buy some penny candies and leave. I frisked him, made him take the bars back, and asked the manager to call the police. He didn't want to, but I made him. Unless one is consistent a child cannot be helped. It is called tough love. Yes, it does make stress, but the stress of letting the child grow up badly is worse. Eddie had to spend two years at St. Mary's Home for Boys to learn how to manage this stealing habit, and other issues as well.

When Eddie was grown up, twenty or so years old and married, he landed in jail for an upaid ticket. He knew his wife had no money to bail him out, so he called me and said, "Mom, will you bail me out?"

"Who chose to get a traffic ticket?

"I did, Mom."

"Who chose to drive and ignore the ticket?

"I did, Mom."

"OK, it's your problem. I can't bail you out. I love you, honey. Good-bye." It's called tough love, and it works. He never did it again.

I look back and ask, "Was it worth it? Twenty-some years of stress?" Yes, with God's help we made it. Oh, we are not finished yet; we will continue to mentor these adult children. But we know they belong to the human race. Yes, they were damaged badly by their birth parents, who gave them a very bad inheritance from drugs, but with God's help and all the medical breakthroughs our society can offer, we will hold our heads high and keep on trying, remembering we are not alone. He promised to be with us until the end of time. And who knows, He might even have that handy spaceship waiting on my front porch…just in case.

CHAPTER 9

Miracles

Miracles! Miracles! Life is full of miracles, but sometimes they go unrecognized. I was very aware that God gave us many in raising these three children.

In the '70s you did not ask to adopt a child who was in foster care. "We don't do it that way" is the answer you got. When we got that answer my heart was saying, "Move over and let God do His thing." We did all the paperwork, had our house checked, our income verified as sufficient to raise a child, etc., and adopted one who was in foster care. That was the first miracle.

When we got Tony we had plans to travel to California with Marcos's parents, who were coming from Peru to visit us for the first time. The agency said, "You can't take Tony outside the state." We had planned this trip for two months. (His biological parents had months left to get their act together before they would lose their parental rights.) I said, "We're taking him; just give me the papers to fill out." Usually papers from the state take months. They gave me the papers. This was miracle number two.

Six months after we had Tony, we got a call about adopting a girl, but we only had one week to decide. Marcos didn't feel ready and was very resistant.

Then the medical foster parent who had taken care of Tony called and asked to talk to Marcos, not me. I gave him the phone and left the room. When he finished the call he came to me and said, "We'll take her." This was indeed a miracle. If you knew Marcos you would understand. So we welcomed Terri.

In the next six months we got Eddie, who was Tony's biological brother. Eddie was in a failed adoption. Two older children were mean to him at his first adoption home. Out of the blue Miriam connected with the adoptive mother, who was going to return Eddie to the agency. She asked if we wanted him. She knew he was Tony's brother. The adoption agency called and asked if we wanted Eddie. How could we say no to another miracle?

I knew from my work in child therapy how important it is for children to put closure on the past and to heal. I was well aware that the agencies at that time were most reluctant to give out any information about a child's past, so I was delighted one day when we were at McDonald's and Tony said, looking over at a family, "Mama, I know those people!"

"Let's go say hello to them," I said. We did. They hugged and high-fived and laughed. We put the tables together and ate together. Tony had been with them but was given to us when they got a new baby. This meeting gave closure. "Thank you, God."

When Eddie told me about those bad, bad people behind us in church and I explained that we never had to see them again, he was vastly relieved, and it was such a good moment of healing.

Terri's mother had moved her from many foster homes. When Terri was about five my medical foster parent, Miriam, met Terri's previous foster parents in a doctor's office. We made contact with them and invited them to Terri's fifth birthday party. (She had no roots and a terrible sense of insecurity.) This small social event gave Terri closure and some healing.

I felt good about all these little miracles.

There was a stand of trees, rocks, and bushes down the street behind our house, some thirty feet in depth. Tony and Eddie called it their forest. At five years of age Eddie kept disappearing in the "forest." One side bordered a 600-foot rock drop-off. They never fell off. Angels kept them safe. One time Tony said, "Dad, come see our forest." They knew all the safe places. Marcos was amazed by this trek.

When Tony was ten he started picking up cigarette butts and smoking them. We worked at getting him to stop, but again, lack of frontal brain development does not allow for correct reasoning. The miracle was that he never got sick.

Because of shooting off his loud mouth Tony had many kids who were his enemies and would do mean tricks, so he took to hiding knives in trees to defend himself against these children. That no one was seriously hurt during these episodes is a first-class miracle.

Both Tony and Eddie, who had no smarts about danger, took to jumping off the roof of our two-story house. Neither one got hurt. God heard our prayers and must have had an extra fleet of angels working for their safety.

Eddie was always using fire to make something. He built one under his bed, but I came upon it before any damage occurred.

In their impulsive effort to be creative, fire seemed to be a fun but dangerous product to use. Both Tony and Eddie would poke sticks in the pilot light and go about setting fires. When they made the bonfire under the pine tree and used lighter fluid to get it going, that they didn't go up in smoke was indeed miraculous. I felt that they kept a number of saints and angels busy, not to mention their parents.

When he around nine Tony got in with some kids who drank. I caught them in the bushes drinking vodka. We got him out of that before it was too late. God was giving us miracles on every corner.

Both boys used staple guns to shoot at each other and their friends, and no one was maimed for life. Wow! Chalk that one up.

There were numerous scrapes with the neighbors. Because drug affected children lag behind peers in their social emotional development there are often poorly read social cues which resulted in arguments, inappropriate words, and many times fights. Sometimes adults in the neighborhood were using inappropriate words which added more fuel to an already out of control situation. At one point we had to limit where our children could play as did neighbors who were near our house.

When I worked at school as a counselor and my own were in school I asked God, "Please take care of my children as I take care of other people's now." And God did. I asked God to let His angels daily take care of them.

One time when Eddie was in kindergarten I saw him in my mind while I was at a meeting, He was sitting on the front step of our house. He was supposed to be in daycare. I asked to leave and rushed home. He said, "I came home, and you weren't here." The note to daycare was still pinned on his jacket. A lovely miracle!

Eddie was sexually abused in daycare. He pleaded, "Don't make me go to daycare. Don't make me take a nap." This is when the predator did his dirty work. I could tell by his face that something was wrong, but he didn't want to talk. Finally I managed to get out of him that the guy working in daycare said if he told anyone he would come at night and kill his whole family. It took six months of counseling before he began to heal. Time with Eddie in my playroom at school helped him tremendously.

Eddie's efforts to duplicate a blowgun with a straw and a sewing pin backfired. He inhaled when he went to blow the pin and swallowed it. I called the doctor, and Eddie had to eat bread and potatoes. The miracle was that he eliminated it without getting his innards poked.

When they were in middle school, after the babysitter had them in bed they would get up at midnight and sneak out with lawn chairs to watch movies at the drive-in theater, down the street. They went out through the window. The miracle was that no one got hurt or picked up for curfew violation.

When Tony was fourteen he was riding Eddie's bike and another boy jumped him and stole the bike. Tony was so angry that he was not coherent. He came home, grabbed a butcher knife, and yelled, "I'm going to get him."

I prayed hard, "Jesus, keep them all safe." The knife, the boy, and the bike came back intact. Glorious miracle.

When Terri danced down the hall at six years of age and whacked her arm into the wall so hard she broke it, I took her to the hospital and wanted to stay with her. (I stayed with all my children; they were afraid of being left.) The doctor did not allow it. They quizzed her on how it happened. She had already told them, but they didn't believe her because of possible child abuse. This second time she never changed her story, replying angrily, "I already told you." After we left and she explained what had happened I realized why they had me leave. A nice miracle.

Probably the worst incident was when Tony hauled off and slugged the girl in the swimming pool because he didn't like the way she looked at him. He was fourteen and a half at the time. We had to go to court. We didn't get sued but had the judge put Tony in St. Mary's Home for Boys for two years. It cost $600 a month to keep him there; we didn't have the money, but the miracle was that there was an adoption assistance program that helped us. We leaned heavily on God, and He was always there.

Tony ran away from an alternative program when he was seventeen, joined a gang, and lived on the street. The miracle was that he didn't end up dead, because leaving a gang was very difficult to do.

Miracles are still happening in my life, in my husband's life, in the lives of our three grown children and grandchildren. I thank God, and I pray that someday we can rid our world of death-dealing drugs and save children from such a miserable existence. I believe there is more good than evil in our world and that by working together we can do wonders and keep the miracles coming.

CHAPTER 10
Lifetime Issues Resulting from Drug Use

As was mentioned earlier, the gap between chronological age and social, emotional, and mental development grows wider as the child becomes an adult. Even such a simple thing as negotiating with the DMV for an emissions check or license renewal can be traumatic. The public does not have a clue that this adult is brain damaged and cannot follow simple steps.

I discovered I had to be there and guide both boys through each step or they would end up in a shouting match, totally confused. I would sit down with them, study the manual, and then go to the DMV and make sure they followed through. I have worked enough with Tony that he can now fill out his own driver's license application. I might add that people willing to devote themselves as mentors to these grown-up drug-affected people need to have the patience of Job.

Neither son can handle directions on the phone. They need to see the person's face, and they need one step at a time. I became a social secretary for both sons. To do any kind of insurance work or anything over the phone was like trying to pour fifty gallons of water through a straw. It just didn't work.

Because of the multiple privacy rules I had to get a note signed by a notary public to help my grandchildren and children.

Tony has his three boys living with him, and I help him parent them. Because Tony has reactive attachment disorder he is not capable of handling many little situations. He cannot separate his feelings from disciplining his children. He tends to start yelling if things go wrong. Tony complained to me, "They're not minding me."

"Give me an example."

"I told Louie to get off his bike and come in here. He's not doing it."

"What you have to do is go out and stand by him and say, 'Get off your bike.' Take his hand and let him know he has to come in. They are at a stage where they need to be walked through what you want them to do."

Tony took a parenting class, but when it was finished he said, "Mom, I've learned more from you."

"Another thing. If you alienate them by screaming you will lose them. They will not listen. They will turn off completely. Don't expect them to do things unless you walk through it with them."

"Tony, remember when you were little and you stashed jam and bread in the doghouse because you were going to run away?"

"Yeah, I remember."

"Well, the bread got stale and the jam wasn't covered, and the doghouse was a mess of bugs and vermin."

"Yes."

"Remember I told you that you had to clean it up, and you made a big fuss?"

"Yes."

Then I said, "OK, who made this mess?"

"I did, Mom."

"All right; you need to go get cleaning stuff and I'll help you if you get stuck. Remember, when we make a mess we clean it. Now as an adult remember with your own children it is important to have them clean up their own messes, without any yelling or screaming."

Sometimes these children will learn a little from past mistakes. As an adult Tony was not willing to follow the rules of our house, so he slept on the street and joined a gang. Then one night he called me and said it was cold sleeping under newspapers. Could he come home?

"Are you willing to follow our rules? No liquor? No smoking?"

"No."

"Well then, you can't come here. What will you do?"

"I'll figure it out."

He stayed for a while with some friends, and when that wore out he looked for a new place. Later he made some poor choices and married.

Neither child can handle credit cards or checkbooks or money. I need to take care of all finances, which I do. Tony is an impulsive spender and has to have his money rationed out to him or there wouldn't be any left for bills and legitimate expenses.

Terri can handle her own money but has many social problems resulting from being abandoned in childhood and sexually abused. When living got tough she turned to drugs to calm the pain and escape.

Because of their limited abilities these adults have a mountain of problems, such as not being able to fill out a form correctly, not keeping past information that will be needed later, and being easily cheated because they don't understand what they are signing.

One of my sons was injured on the job and was told by his boss to lie to the hospital and say the injury wasn't on the job. His boss said he would pay the bill. Of course he didn't pay the bill, and Eddie is stuck with a monstrous bill. A normal person would know enough not to lie, but these adults don't have this ability. It takes a while to see that one can't assume anything with these children in their grown-up bodies.

Dishonest business people took advantage of them; one son was told one wage and then the check reflected another number. The employer was smart enough to see that Tony couldn't afford a lawyer to get his just wage.

The part that is most difficult to deal with is that there are multiple issues, not just drugs, in each child's life. Tony has the loss of being abandoned, the trauma that comes from being neglected, the pain of drugs in his mom, obsessive compulsive disorder, retroactive attachment disorder, and ADHD. Add all this baggage to drug abuse in-utero and you have an awfully heavy load.

Terri and Eddie were also sexually abused. This robs a child of his or her soul. It takes an awful lot of help and counseling to restore some minimum of emotional health. As a parent, teacher, or counselor one has to deal with all of these issues.

I pray that God will give me good health to live long enough to see my grandchildren grow up as good citizens. Just the other day one grandson said to me, "Grandma, don't ever die; we need you." I also trust that when I am gone God will finish the work we began with these children who were given such a bad start on this planet. I have confidence that there are more good people than misguided people and that His Spirit will work through them to renew, refresh, and bring about a society that has compassion for those marginalized.

We were greatly blessed with many wonderful teachers, counselors, doctors, and mental health workers and friends to help us in our parenting journey.

Printed in the United States
By Bookmasters